Volume 1 Number 1   Spring 1978

PAPERBACK QUARTERLY

"A JOURNAL FOR PAPERBACK COLLECTORS"

Contents

The Pecan Valley Press
Brownwood, Texas

The Paperback Quarterly will feature articles and notes dealing with every type (mystery, science fiction, detective, western, adventure, etc.) and with every aspect of new, old, and rare paperbacks. Emphasis will be placed on the historical research of paperbacks, their authors, illustrators, publishers, and distribution; but the editors also invite contributions of bibliographical interest. In short, the only criterion for the editor's consideration is that the subject matter pertain only to paperbacks. In addition to articles and notes, the PQ will feature a section for the review of both old and new paperback originals.

The PQ will be published in March, June, September, and December of each year with a subscription rate of $4.00 per year or individual copies at $1.25 each.

All correspondence, articles, notes, queries, book reviews or books for review, and subscriptions should be sent to: 1710 Vincent, Brownwood, Texas 76801

Billy C. Lee............. Co-Editor
Charlotte Laughlin....... Co-Editor
Bill Crider.............. Contributing Editor
Fred Sylvester........... Technical Director
Tessica Martin........... Photographer

Paperback Originals
------Bill Crider

The paperback original as we know it was born in
1950. Even at that time, of course, there was nothing
new in the idea of original fiction in paper covers,
as those familiar with Beadle's nickel, dime, and fif-
teen cent novels know. Beadle's books first appeared
nearly one hundred years before 1950. And even in the
1940s novels appeared in paper covers without first
having gone through higher-priced, cloth-bound editions.
Many of these, however, were published by small houses,
were digest size (HandiBooks, for example), and did
not really resemble the reprints being issued by Pocket
Books, Bantam, Avon, and others.

The new history of paperback original publishing
began quietly in late 1949 with a brief article in the
December 3 issue of Publisher's Weekly stating that
"Beginning in February [1950], original fiction including westerns and mysteries will be published at 25
cents in a pocket-size format by Fawcett Publications."[1]
The series, to be called Gold Medal Books, had actually
already begun with two "experimental titles," both
anthologies of material culled from two Fawcett magazines. The titles were The BEST of TRUE MAGAZINE and
The Best of TODAY'S WOMAN.[2]

This announcement does not seem to have caused any
undue excitement, and there was no further news of Fawcett's venture in Publisher's Weekly until May 13, 1950,
when another brief article appeared. This article said
that Fawcett books were "similar in appearance and cover
allure to many of the paperback reprints, but the story
material [was]original and not reprinted from regular
editions."[3] (The key word here is "regular." "Regular"
editions were cloth-bound. Pocket-size books were reprints of "regular" editons. Therefore paper originals
could never be "regular.") The authors of these fiction
originals were to be paid a $2000 advance against a
guaranteed first printing of 200,000 copies. The May,
1950, Fawcett releases, actually the first four Gold
Medal novels, were Stretch Dawson by W. R. Burnett
(author of Little Caesar), Nude in Mink by Sax Rohmer

(creator of Fu Manchu), I'll Find You by Richard
Himmel, and The Persian Cat by John Flagg. Burnett's
book was a western; the latter three books were mys-
tery/adventure novels.[4]

Such a publishing method seems natural, almost
inevitable, to us now, when original paperback novels
make up some of the greatest successes of the publishing year (such as Pyramid's best-selling and widely
imitated Bicentennial series by John Jakes, or Avon's
Wicked Loving Lies, a romance which sold close to 300,
000 copies in its first month of publication). In
1950, however, paper-covered books existed primarily
to reprint the higher-priced hardcover editions, and
it was not long before what Publisher's Weekly called
a "spirited debate" broke out between Fawcett and the
other publishing houses, most notably Pocket Books,
a pioneer reprint firm.[5] Freeman Lewis, executive
vice-president of Pocket Books, said that "'*Success
ful* authors are not interested in original publishing
at 25 cents.'"[6] Mr. Lewis went on to say that while
many works were no doubt available for original publishing, these were "mostly rejects, or sub-standard
books by usually competent writers."[7]

There was also a financial side to the debate.
From the 25-cent originals, the author got the entire
royalty. If his book was first published in a "regular"
edition, the author had to split the reprint royalty
50-50 with the hardcover publisher. Of course, as
these publishers were quick to point out, the paperback writer was left without the normal royalties paid
on the hardcover edition and whatever book club rights
he might have received. There was also a strong impli-
cation by the hardback publishers that paperback writers would be unlikely ever to make a movie sale.[8]

Fawcett responded that its original novels were
equal in quality to other 25-cent books (i.e., reprints)
and mentioned that among its authors were many who had
first published with some success in hard covers, including Rohmer, Burnett, MacKinlay Kantor, and Octavus
Roy Cohen. As for finances, Fawcett felt that the author's reward came much more promptly from original
paperback publishing than from the hardcover firms.

In addition, at least one original had already been
sold to the movies, thus increasing the author's bene-
fits. (That exemplary title was The Violent Ones by
Howard Hunt, a best-selling writer of the late 1940s
and 1950s, who wrote paperbacks under his own name and
several pseudonyms--Gordon Davis, Robert Dietrich,
David St. John--and later achieved fame in other areas.)
All in all, Fawcett concluded that there were plenty of
action, adventure, and western manuscripts to go around
and that its original-publishing operation was "no
threat" to the reprint or hardcover firms.[9] This was
clearly not the view of LeBaron R. Barker of Doubleday,
who felt that original paperback could "'undermine the
whole structure of publishing.'"[10] The "spirited debate" grew even more acrimonious. Donald MacCampbell,
a literary agent, wrote in a letter to Publisher's
Weekly that one publisher "threatened to boycott my
agency if it continued to negotiate contracts with
original 25-cent firms."[11]

What was all the shouting about? For one thing,
Gold Medal titles were selling quite a few copies. As
Ralph Daigh, Editorial Director of Gold Medal, put it,
"In the past six months we have produced 9,020,645 books
and people seem to like them very well."[12] Gold Medal
was a success, and its output increased from thirty-five
titles in 1950 to sixty-six in 1951.[13] It was obvious
that the other publishers saw that Gold Medal was both
cutting into their market and creating its own market.
They seemed both envious and resentful, and most soon
realized that they would have to meet the competition.
Publisher's Weekly reported in May, 1952, that Avon
had included three originals in its April, 1952, releases and was "looking for more manuscripts." Dell
was "'thinking about' some systematic program of original publishing." Lion Books had "a definite original
publishing program in the works." Graphic had begun
"publishing originals on a systematic basis almost a
year ago." Bantam, Pocket, and NAL stood firm, saying
that they would "not be competing in this field."[14]
(It is interesting that Arnold Hano of Lion Books saw
fit to respond to this Article with a letter stating
that "The original publishing program of Lion Books is

a supplement, and merely a supplement, to our reprint program."[15]

One clever attempt to circumvent the original/reprint controversy was made in 1952 by Ian Ballantine, founder of Ballantine books. His idea was "to offer trade publishers a plan for simultaneous publishing of original titles in two editions, a hard-cover 'regular' edition for bookstore sale, and a paper-cover, newsstand-size, low-priced edition for mass market sale."[16] One of Ballantine's first, and very successful, titles was Cameron Hawley's Executive Suite.[17]

Another unique development in 1952 was the A. A. Wyn company's series, Ace Double Novel Books. Each Ace Double Novel included two books, one reprint and one original work, and had two "front" covers and two title pages, a bibliographer's nightmare come true. These books sold for 35 cents. The first Ace Double featured The Grinning Gizmo by Samuel W. Taylor (reprint) and Too Hot For Hell by Keith Vining (original).[18]

In 1953, Dell finally announced its plans for Dell First Editions.[19] Dell had for some time been planning the expansion of its paperback program and had previously announced that "originals [would] play a large part in the expansion."[20] Early titles in the series included Walt Grove's Down, Frederic Brown's Madball, and Charles Einstein's The Bloody Spur, later filmed and reprinted as While The City Sleeps. Dell's program, like Fawcett's, was very successful; the practice of publishing paperback originals was well established.

Some notably successful paperback writers include John D. MacDonald, John Jakes, Kurt Vonnegut, Jr., and Kathleen E. Woodiwiss. MacDonald began writing for Gold Medal in the arly 1950s and also did originals for Dell First Editions and Popular Library. He has seen his popular Travis McGee series of paper originals reprinted in hardcover and has lately achieved best-seller status in "regular" editons, most recently with Condominium. Kurt Vonnegut's second novel, The Sirens of Titan was a Dell First Edition, and he also published Mother Night with Gold Medal. A book club has recently reprinted all five volumes of John Jakes' Bicentennial series in hardcover editions, available to members of

the club either in separate volumes of as a set. Kathleen E. Woodiwiss has been so successful that Avon issued her latest book, Shanna, in a trade edition for
$3.95. No doubt a standard size paperback, somewhat
cheaper, will be issued later. This latter development
seems to have brought originals almost full circle:
the pocket-size edition of Shanna will be a reprint of
a higher-priced original.

Notes

[1] Publisher's Weekly, December 3, 1949, p. 2282.

[2] Ibid.

[3] "First 25-Cent Gold Medal Originals Published,"
Publisher's Weekly, May 13, 1950, p. 2064.

[4] Ibid.

[5] "Debate About Original Fiction In 25-Cent Paper
Editions," Publisher's Weekly, October 21, 1950, p. 1840.

[6] Ibid., p. 1841.

[7] Ibid., p. 1842.

[8] Ibid., p. 1841.

[9] Ibid., p. 1842.

[10] Ibid., p. 1841.

[11] Publisher's Weekly, November 18, 1950, p. 2198.

[12] Ibid., p. 2199.

[13] "Publishers Issued 11, 255 Titles, Including
More Fiction, in 1951," Publisher's Weekly, January
19, 1952, p. 195.

[14] "original Paperback Publishing Grow; Its Merits
and Effects Are Debated," Publisher's Weekly, May 3,
1952, pp. 1831-2.

[15] Publisher's Weekly, May 17, 1952, p. 1995.

[16] "Plan for Simultaneous Issue of Hard and Paper
Originals Stirs Discussion," Publisher's Weekly, May
17, 1952, p. 1993.

[17] "Ballantine Announces Titles, Staff Members,
New Address," Publisher's Weekly, September 6, 1952,
p. 912.

[18] "Pocket-Sized Books Launched by A. A. Wyn,"
Publisher's Weekly, Octover 18, 1952, pp. 1719-20.

[19] "Tips for the Bookseller," Publisher's Weekly,

May 30, 1953, p. 2219.
    20"You Meet Such Interesting People," <u>Publisher's</u>
<u>Weekly</u>, November 1, 1952, p. 1883.

Marijuana, music, and murder made him...

TOO HOT FOR HELL

Keith Vining

ACE DOUBLE NOVEL BOOKS 35¢

An ACE Original

Paperback Writers
------Bill Crider

There are writers whose works sell millions of
copies; yet their names are scarcely known in literary
circles, and their books receive little or no critical
attention. These are the writers of paperback originals,
and the purpose of this column is to talk about their
work, to tell who they are and what they've done. It
will be written in a personal and informal style because I'll be sticking pretty closely to my own particular enthusiasms (and they are many) among these writers.
    I'd like to devote this first excursion to a writer
named Harry Whittington, most of whose work has appeared
under his own name, but who has also published as Whit
Harrison, Hallam Whitney, Hondo Wells, Steve Phillips,
Harriett Katheryn Myers, Kel Holland, Clay Stuart, Harry
White, and (most recently) Ashley Carter. He has done
paperback originals for Handi-Books, Ace, Gold Medal,
Carnival, Beacon, Avon, Belmont, and Pyramid, among
others. These originals include mysteries, suspense
stories, westerns, "backwoods" novels, war tales, movie
novelizations, "straight" novels, nurse stories, and
"plantation" books. In short, Whittington has done
just about everything except (as far as I know) science
fiction. And he's done it well, which is what really
counts, because he's a fine storyteller.
    I've never picked up any Whittington book of any
kind and been disappointed in the story. He knows how
to keep you turning the pages, and to me this is the
primary virtue in anyone's writing. He also does a
solid job of characterization, not by avoiding stereo-
types entirely but by changing them to suit his own ends.
    A good example of Whittington's use of story and
character can be found in Slay Ride for a Lady (Handi-
Books, 1950). Here he relies on a plot outline that
has been popular since at least the time of The Odyssey:
a man has a goal which seems within easy reach; suddenly,
unexpected complications arise, and things get worse,
then worse still, and even worse. This is a formula
which Whittington used again and again, almost always
with success. And Slay Ride is a success. Dan Hender-

son, ex-cop framed for murder, is released from prison
to find the wife of Henry Nelson, crime and political
big-shot. He finds her. She is immediately murdered.
Framed again, beaten to a pulp by vicious cops, betrayed
by a girl he trusts, Henderson nevertheless prevails.
But there's no phony happy ending, no boy-gets-girl.
It wouldn't fit with a book this tough, and Whittington
spares us the falseness.

Slay Ride is obviously in the tough tradition, and
Henderson survives incredible physical punishment with
scarcely time out to eat or sleep, a fact which fans of
the genre will not find objectionable. The style is
lean and laconic, with the following neat exchange between Henderson and the woman he's been sent to find:

"What's your name?
"Henderson," I said.
"Bill? Frank? Tom?"
"No," I said.

It may appear slightly dated to today's fans, but Slay
Ride for a Lady still delivers a fair share of hardboiled
delights.

An entirely different kind of story is Rapture
Alley (by "Whit Harrison", Carnival, 1953). I don't
know how to classify this book, except to call it a
"contemporary problem" novel. It's about a beautiful
young girl named Lora who moves (pretty quickly) from
whiskey to marijuana to heroin, has an illegitimate
child (by her sick sister's husband), and falls for
a handsome young doctor. I'll admit this sounds pretty
scapy, and I kept looking for easy outs--losing the
baby, marriage to the sister's husband when the sister
dies, marriage to the handsome doctor. But even in
this kind of book Whittington avoids the easy outs.
The baby is born and the sister dies; but the husband
is a louse, and Lora refuses to marry him. The young
doctor turns out to be an addict himself.

Many readers might find this novel a little "soft"
by today's standards, but in 1953 it would probably
have seemed a powerful anti-dope story. The ending is
marred by sentimentality; but while happiness is implied,
it isn't promised. I doubt very much that anyone writing
for the Carnival Books market in 1953 delivered as much

10

as Whittington.

Some of Whittington's best work was done for Fawcett Gold Medal, my own favorites being Web of Murder
and Brute in Brass. To turn to another genre, however,
we might examine Backwoods Tramp (GM, 1959). This is a
"southern-regional" story (Whittington wrote at least
three books with "Backwoods" as part of the title),
featuring the archetypal southern poor-white girl:
"She'd developed suddenly, so even though she looked
swollen and full, she wasn't quite finished." The
hero, Jake Richards, meets her when searching the swamp
country for Marve Pooser, the man who engineered the
robbery which cost Jake his job, his girl, and his rep-
utation. As is often the case, things go from bad to
worse, and then get worse yet. As events resolve themselves, Jake loses the girl; but he learns quite a lot
about himself and his motives, and in the end he's able
to face what he's become and to avoid becoming something
worse.

This is the interesting thing about Whittington's
characters: they aren't static; they learn. Another
good example of this quality can be found in Searching
Rider (Ace Double, 1961). In this western, Hunt Kaylor,
a farmer, rides out after the three killers who murdered
his nine-year-old son. Kaylor's wife pleads with Matt
Logan to go after her husband, who she is certain will
be killed. Logan goes, hating Kaylor more than the
murderers for his stupidity and incompetence. But in
the course of the adventure he comes to admire Kaylor's
persistence in the face of his own fear, his dogged
determination to do at least one thing right or die
trying. Logan learns that he has been wrong about
Kaylor, and even more wrong about his own life, but
fortunately it's not quite too late for Logan to
change.

Most recently, Whittington has been writing as
"Ashley Carter" for Fawcett Gold Medal, producing
"Lance Horner" novels, as they are called on the cover.
These are slave-plantation stories, very much more in
the vein of Mandingo than Gone with the Wind. Master
of Blackoaks (GM, 1976) is the first of a series. All
the Whittington story values are present, spiced up

(or weighed down, depending on your point of view) by a vast assortment of southern gothic family problems (lunacy, homosexuality), sex (regardless of race, creed, or color), and violence (a runaway slave is killed and thrown to the hogs, for example). This seems a far cry from Whittington's early work (which I confess I preferred for its lean, understated style), but it seems to be quite popular and successful, proving once again that a gifted storyteller can work well in almost any field he chooses. I, for one, wish him only the best.

(Readers interested in a Whittington bibliography should check Contemporary Authors which features what appears to be a complete check list of Whittington titles through 1970, some 99 books, mostly paperback originals. Several of the westerns are still in print, but others may be more difficult to find.)

The PQ Interview With:

HARRY WHITTINGTON

PQ: Your first books were for Phoenix (according to
Contemporary Authors). So how did you get started
as a paperback writer?

HW: *The sales to Phoenix were on my own. A friend of
mine, Chicago-based crime writer William T. Brannon,
sold my book Slay Ride for a Lady to Jim Quinn of
Handi-Books. Quinn also published The Brass
Monkey and The Lady Was a Tramp. In 1951, I wrote
and sold 15 paperback novels!*

PQ: You wrote for Ace, Graphic, Handi-Books, and Gold
Medal (among others). How did the requirements
differ from house to house?

HW: *I never found the requirements that different from
house to house. I tried to write the best I could
--my favorite among the contemporary writers at
the time were Fredric C. Davis, Day Keene, Fred
Brown, and if I was influenced by anybody it was by
them--and by James M. Cain. I figured he had the
patent on the lean, hard prose perfect for the
suspense novel. As far as I was concerned, Cain
wrote the clean, lean prose that Hemingway is
revered for.*

PQ: Did you ever find that the hardcover houses held
your paperback work against you?

HW: *Perhaps one lady editor of a very famous hardback
did think paperback writers were less than marvelous. She rejected a book of mine which she said
she liked "because he writes so many paperbacks."
I don't know, any more, about the difference between paperback and hardcover. I suppose prestige
enters into it, and if a hardcover sells well, its
sales in paper are enhanced.*

13

PQ: What is your own favorite among your paperback works? Why?

HW: I always like the novel I'm working on at the moment best. But among all my books I think I like Slay Ride for a Lady because Jim Quinn said he published it because it was the kind of book he'd liked to have written. You'll Die Next made the New York Times call me the "best sheer story teller since the greatest days of the pre-sex detective pulps". Web of Murder got me compared, most favorably to "the early James M. Cain" by the New York Times. Saddle the Storm was praised by the Saturday Review of Literature and was the best paperback western of 1954 according to Western Writers of America.

PQ: Is it true that you are now writing the "Blackoaks" novels for Fawcett under the name of "Ashley Carter"? If so, how did you get this assignment, and how does it differ from your past works?

HW: I became "Ashley Carter" because Harry Whittington didn't sound southern enough for Gold Medal. I got the assignment when Lance Horner, who wrote all the Falconhurst novels except Mandingo died and left The Golden Stud unfinished. I rewrote, finished and edited it, and was asked to continue the series. As Ashley Carter I've done Sword of the Golden Stud (Aug. 77); Master of Blackoaks (July 76); Secret of Blackoaks (March 78) and Panama (scheduled for September 78).

These books differ in many ways from my past works--though I did many "regional" novels-- Backwoods Hussy, Gods Back Was Turned, Woman on the Place, etc. They are longer--they are more extravagant in phrasing, action, reaction, motivation. They are fun to write, and I hope they'll be fun to read.

14

PQ: You've written westerns, mysteries, historicals--
nearly everything. Do you have a favorite genre?
If so, what is it? Why?

HW: *It's hard to answer this. I think the biggest
single mistake--I made many--in my long writing
career was in writing "nearly everything" under
the name Harry Whittington. If a reader bought
a John D. MacDonald, he expected tough suspense
etc. If he bought Frank Bonham, he knew he was
getting a western. If he bought Whittington he
didn't know what in hell he was getting. If I
could do it again--knowing what I do now, I'd be
Hondo Wells (westerns), Ashley Carter (slave-plantation), Hallam Whitney (southern regionals), etc.*

*As to my favorite--I think the reason I wrote
everything--besides going with the needs of the
market at that moment, was that I like any good
and exciting story--western, suspense, mystery,
whatever.*

I've had fun and don't regret anything.

A Conversation with the de Camps
------Charlotte Laughlin

March 7-9, the editors of PQ had the pleasure of
visiting with two of the most distinguished paperback
writers in America. Indeed, to call Catherine Crook
de Camp and L. Sprague de Camp paperback writers is
an understatement. Together they have published
nearly 100 books, both paperback and hardback. The
subjects of their books include engineering, military
history, archeology, natural history, a writers'
manual, children's literature, historical novels,
economics, and their favorite and most popular genre,
science fiction and fantasy.

Mr. de Camp's career began as a technical writer.
He received a M.S. from Stevens Institute of Technology,
in 1933, in the field of aeronautical engineering.
Since there were few jobs available during the Great
Depression, he took what positions he could find as an
educator and technical writer.

Asked by a group of students at Howard Payne
University how he happened to enter fiction writing,
he replied with a wry sense of humor. "The answer is
very simple; in four words, I lost my job. What
happened was that in 1938, I was working for a trade
journal in New York as one of the editors; and I had
written a few stories and articles and sold them on
the side. The publisher decided to economize by firing
the two most junior editors, so I got it in the neck!
He was very apologetic about it, but that didn't do me
any good. However, I thought that now if I spend five
hours writing a week and make so much money, if I could
spend fifty hours at it I would make ten times as much.
Well, there's a fallacy there because you run into the
law of diminishing returns, but I nevertheless took the
plunge and went into freelance writing. And except for
the second World War and a couple of temporary jobs, I've
been at it ever since. I found that I did about as well
financially as I had been doing, I could be my own boss,
and I could wear out all my old clothes."

When asked why he writes, he replied with a story.
"When the second World War came along in 1942, I went

16

to naval headquarters in New York and volunteered for the Naval Reserve. The young officers who were examining me, after beating around the bush (they seemed a little embarrassed), finally said, 'Well, Mr. de Camp, what we really want to know is why you write.' I thought a minute; and I said, 'To make a living.' Then they relaxed, and everything went fine, and I got my commission. And I spent three and a half years navigating a desk and fighting the war with a flashing slide rule along with Isaac Asimov and Robert Heinlein at the Naval Air Materials Center in Philadelphia.

"Well, that was the truthful answer, but it wasn't quite the whole truth. Actually, I also write because I enjoy writing. I enjoy it so much that even if I were working full time at another job, I'd be doing it even if nobody paid me a nickel for it. I enjoy it so such that I say that it's really not fair--I don't work for a living; I just endulge a hobby, and people are silly enough to pay me for it! Also I do like being my own boss and making my own schedule. If you're going to be a full time freelance you have to be a much tougher boss on yourself than any other boss would be to you. I put in something like seventy hours a week of work, and I'm up at 6:00 in the morning. Those don't sound exactly like union hours!"

In 1941, Mr. de Camp's first book of science fiction was published. He said that this book, Lest Darkness Fall, is his favorite of his own science fiction and that it has enjoyed the most reprints of all his books. But since it has been out longer than any of his other science fiction, he said that he is not sure whether or not the number of reprints means that it is the public's favorite of his books.

Whatever the public's opinion may be, Mrs. de Camp is certain that Lest Darkness Fall is her favorite of his books. She explained that she had studied economics and English literature in college and then taught in private girls' schools. When she and Mr. de Camp began dating, he brought her science fiction books to read and asked her opinion of them. She confessed that at first she thought they were absolutely terrible; but she gradually developed a taste for science fiction. Her approval of the genre was assured when the money advanced to Mr. de Camp for <u>Lest Darkness Fall</u> enabled the two of them to get married.

Today Mrs. de Camp manages all of the business aspects of her husband's writing, as well as writing herself. She reveals that even at such a romantic time as their wedding she was a practical business woman. Two days before the wedding Mr. de Camp came to her, quite distraught, and confessed that there was no way that he could complete the manuscript of <u>Lest Darkness Fall</u> before their marriage. Since he was committed to deliver the manuscript to the publishers just one week after their marriage, his need to work was obviously going to interfere with the honeymoon. Being the business woman that she is, Mrs. de Camp assured him that there was nothing to worry about—— they would just take his typewriter with them on the honeymoon; and while he typed, she would shop for furniture for their first home. Unknown to their families, they planned to take a room in a hotel in New York City for a week, finish the manuscript, and then go on a real honeymoon. But their families found them out, laughed Mrs. de Camp. After the wedding, they drove across town, checked in a hotel, and went downstairs to have dinner in the hotel restaurant. Of the hundreds of hotels in New York City, their families had chosen this one as the place for an after-the-wedding dinner together. "But they were more embarrassed than we were," said Mrs. de Camp. "And we didn't explain to them why we were still in town, instead of being on our honeymoon trip as originally planned. But it didn't matter," she added. "After he finished the manuscript, we had a lovely honeymoon."

Mrs. de Camp said that her career outside her home was brought to an abrupt halt when she married. "The headmistress at the school where I taught was very straight-laced, so much so that she required her teachers to wear hats and gloves when they went out. And when I married she didn't want me anymore because she didn't allow any of her teachers to be married." At this point Mr. de Camp broke in with his characteristic humor. "Everyone knows what married people do!"

As Mr. de Camp's writing career expanded, his wife assumed more and more of the responsibilities for bookkeeping, filing, and financial affairs, in addition to taking care of their home and their two sons. She also began serving as a proofreader for her husband's manuscripts until she finally became the co-author of many books with him. She joked that her move from business manager and proofreader to co-author was an attempt to stay in good physical shape. "I had to write in self-defense. In those days, good ladies gave tea parties for struggling young authors. We would go to these parties (of course, they had to invite me); and they would all flutter around Sprague saying, 'Oh, Mr. de Camp, what do you do?' and so forth. I would be left standing almost alone at the tea table, and I nibbled sandwich after sandwich, and I began to get terribly fat. So I thought, 'I've got to to something to save my figure.' Then it came to me one day, that if I write a book, they'll flutter around me, and I won't get to the tea table, and I'll keep my shape. So I wrote a book, and it worked, and I still have something left of a shape. Well, whether that's entirely true or not, that's my story; and I stick to it!"

Besides the books written with her husband, Mrs. de Camp has written several books entirely on her own. Her training in economics and practical business experience resulted in the paperback original The Money Tree, published by New American Library in 1972. As a paperback original, it never received the attention that it deserved from reviewers--(an all too common problem, which the PQ hopes to remedy when we have more people contributing to the reviews in this journal.) However, The Money Tree did attract the attention of the U.S. News and World Report publishers, which commissioned her to write a book entitled Teach Your Child to Manage Money, published in 1975. This book was misinterpreted as recommending that every child be given a minimum allowance of $5.00 per week. Because of the furor raised by this misinterpretation, she was featured on the cover of The National Enquirer and interviewed on television by Barbara Walters.

Today she has turned her independent efforts to writing science fiction for children. Her book, <u>Creatures of the Cosmos</u>, is currently available; and she is working on others.

Together Mr. and Mrs. de Camp are researching a biography of the science fiction and fantasy author, Robert E. Howard. This work accounted for their recent visit to Brownwood and surrounding towns. They looked through Howard's books which are housed in the Howard Payne Library; visited with residents of Cross Plains, particularly Jack Scott the award-winning former editor of the Cross Plains newspaper; and interviewed other people in the area who had known Robert E. Howard. They also planned a trip to Baird to check the records concerning Howard in the Callahan County courthouse; but since I had already made photocopies of those records for an independent project for PQ, I was able to share with them and save them that trip. In return, they graciously consented to give an informal interview for the PQ and to speak to my English classes about writing and research. These talks are the basis of this article.

Mr. de Camp explained that he was introduced to the works of Robert E. Howard by the Swedish business-man, Bjorn Nyberg, who had written <u>The Return of Conan</u> to improve his English. Since then, the two men have worked together to publish that book (1955) and to produce <u>Conan the Avenger</u> (1967) in the Ace series of Conan novels. Mr. de Camp was immediately impressed with Howard's style of writing, which he and Mrs. de Camp described as having a biblical roll. He explained that when he is writing a Conan novel or story, he prepares to imitate Howard's style by rereading parts of the King James Version of the Bible and by rereading <u>Conan the Conqueror</u>, which is his favorite of Howard's books and which was first given to him in 1950, by Fletcher Pratt. In passing, Mr. de Camp commented that to improve any sort of writing style he recommended reading all of the King James Version of the Bible, all of the works of Shakespeare, and all of Burton's <u>Arabian Nights</u>; he added that if anyone hoped to write science fiction he should read all of ancient mythology. He interrupted himself to say that all of these recom-

mendations are found in Science-Fiction Handbook.
While speaking of writing style, Mr. de Camp said
that his own has been influenced by the works of
Thorne Smith, Ernest Hemingway, P.G. Wodehouse, and
of course, Robert E. Howard.

Interest in Howard's works led to the forma-
tion of Conan Properties, a holding company composed
of the New York Lawyer, Arthur M. Lieberman, and three
directors: John Troll, a patent engineer; Glenn Lord,
the author of The Last Celt, a bio-bibliography of
Robert E. Howard; and L. Sprague de Camp himself. The
holding company was necessary to clarify who had what
rights to the name and character of Conan. When Robert
E. Howard committed suicide in 1936, his works were
considered to have very little value. In fact, the
probate of his estate mentioned only $1,000 from a life
insurance policy made out to his mother, who survived
him by only a few hours; $702 in First National Bank
of Brownwood, Texas; $1,850 in Postal Deposits in the
Brownwood Post Office, and "One 1935 Model, Standard
Chevrolet Sedan, appraised at $350." When Howard's
father died, he left the undervalued manuscripts to a
Dr. Kuykendall and his family of Ranger, Texas. Dr.
Kuykendall did not live to enjoy the financial rewards
of the materials either; but when Glenn Lord became the
literary agent for Dr. Kuykendall's wife and daughter,
he actively began to market Howard's work. Howard's
name and characters became very valuable; and the
holding company, Conan Properties, was needed to protect
everyone's interests.

The value of the character Conan can be seen in two
recent undertakings. Conan Properties granted Paramount
Pictures the right to produce a Conan movie, for which
Mr. de Camp is a technical advisor. Bantam Books, Inc.
entered a contract to produce six new Conan books. The
first one, Conan the Swordsman, consists of several
short stories and one long article. It was delivered
to the publishers in December and will come out this
July. The second book in the Bantam series, Conan the
Liberator, will be written by Lin Carter and Mr. de Camp
together. At present several chapters are completed.
Karl Edward Wagner is under contract to write three of
the books in this series.

Despite all of these other activities, Mr. de Camp and his colleague Dr. Jane Griffin have the Robert E. Howard biography in the beginning marketing stage. They have completed sample chapters and a synopsis, which they will show to interested publishers. The editors and readers of PQ will be eagerly awaiting the appearance of this biography of a great science fiction and fantasy writer, by a great science fiction and fantasy writer.

Robert E. Howard's Library:
An Annotated Checklist
------Charlotte Laughlin

Before Robert Ervin Howard committed suicide in
June of 1936, he had distinguished himself as a writer
of fiction for pulp magazines. During his lifetime,
none of his works were published in book form, paperback or otherwise; but within two years of his death,
two books of his writings had appeared; and the "Cheap
Edition" (1938), cited but unseen by Glenn Lord, of
A Gent From Bear Creek was probably a paperback. The
cheaper paper binding would account for the five shilling
difference in price. After 1938, Howard was almost
forgotten by everyone but the strongest devotees of
pulp fiction. In 1946, a book of Howard's poems was
published; but it was not until the 1950 Gnome Press
appearance of Conan the Conqueror that a new generation
of readers received a taste of the vigor and imagination
in Howard's fiction.

Since that first taste, the public's appetite for
his writings has been insatiable. Today there are
dozens of Howard books and take-offs or extentions of
his works available both in hardback and paperback. No
less than five paperback publishers have recently made
Howard books available. Berkeley Medallion has published several books by Howard, boldly advertised as
"By the Creator of CONAN." The popularity of his
character, Conan, accounts for the numerous books
released by Ace Books. Fragments of Conan stories
were completed by such writers as L. Sprague de Camp,
Lin Carter, and Bjorn Nyberg. These writers also
filled in the "life story" of Conan with novels of
their own, based on the Howard character. A similar
approach has been taken by Zebra Books which has
released some original Howard books and some books
by writers such as David C. Smith, Richard Tierney,
and Andrew J. Offutt, but based on the Howard characters, Cormac Mac Art and Brak Mak Morn. Warner Books
has released a series of books also based on a Howard
character; in this case Karl Edward Wagner is completing
the "life story" and exploits of Kane. Finally, Bantam
has contracted to publish six new Conan books, the

23

first of which, <u>Conan the Swordwman</u>, will be released
in July of this year.

With all the attention paid to Howard by paperback publishers and readers, he is a fitting subject for
a PQ article. In this issue I well present a partial
checklist of the books in Robert E. Howard's personal
library, which were presented to the Howard Payne
College Library in June of 1936. Not all of the books
which were originally presented are still preserved,
however; and some books which did not belong to Howard
were added in his memory. A short history of the
Robert E. Howard Memorial Collection will show how
difficult it is to draw critical conclusions from
what is presently available.

The establishment of the Robert E. Howard Memorial
Collection was announced on Monday, June 29, 1936, in
<u>The Brownwood Bulletin</u>, under the headline, "Library
of Late Robert E. Howard Is Given to Howard Payne
College."

> Howard Payne College received last week
> from Dr. I. M. Howard of Cross Plains the gift
> of the library of his son, Robert E. Howard,
> former Howard Payne student, whose death
> occurred recently.
>
> The library consists of some 300 books,
> the great majority of which deal with history
> and biography. More than 50 volumes of cur-
> rent drama and poetry also are included in
> the collection.
>
> Along with the books, the college
> acquired a complete file of all the magazines
> which carry the literary contributions of
> Robert E. Howard. Included in this file are
> short stories, novelettes and book length
> novels and many poems.
>
> The library is being prepared for
> cataloguing and circulation and is to be
> known as "The Robert E. Howard Memorial
> Collection."
>
> Efforts are being made by the friends
> of the late author to augment the collection

by regular contributions. An effort also
is being made to collect and publish a
volume of young Howard's poems.

In retrospect, it appears that although the
library staff gratefully cataloged the books, they
saw little value in the pulp magazines. Today the
accession records of the Howard Payne Library show
that nearly 300 books were cataloged for the Robert
E. Howard Memorial Collection, but there are no
records that the magazines were ever cataloged.
Eventually Dr. Howard reclaimed his son's magazines;
but since he believed that the books were receiving
proper care, he left them in the library.

Two stories have circulated around Howard Payne
concerning Dr. Howard's reasons for reclaiming the
magazines. The story told by Dr. Howard and recounted
by Glenn Lord in The Last Celt is that too many students were allowed to use the magazines, which were
literally being read to pieces. A Cross Plains resi-
dent adds that some articles had even been cut out of
the magazines and that Dr. Howard felt that it was
necessary for him to take back the magazines in order
to preserve them. A second story, told by a woman who
was teaching English at Howard Payne in 1936, places
the cause of the withdrawal of the magazines not on
overuse, but on neglect. The woman who was the librarian
at Howard Payne in 1936, told the English teacher that
she did not think that the pulp magazines had any place
in the library of a Christian college. She was offended,
like many people before and after her, by the scenes of
violence and scantily clad women depicted on the covers.
She said that she placed these magazines in the basement
of the administration building, now known as Old Main.
When Dr. Howard learned that they were in a damp basement, he boxed them up and took them home with him.

Which story is the correct one cannot be deter-
mined. Dr. Howard might have falsified the story some-
what in order to conceal the fact that his son's work
had been deemed morally unfit for a Christian library.
I can think of no reason, however, why a librarian
would have told a lie to make it appear that she

were the cause of a loss to the college when she really
was not. Of course, the truth may be a combination of
the two stories. Perhaps the librarian placed the
western and fight magazines, which she would have
regarded as less offensive, where they could be read
by students; and perhaps the magazines really could
not stand the wear and tear. While these magazines
may have been being overused, the fantasy pulps with
their sensational covers may have lain mouldering in
the basement of the building in which I now teach.

     After the first few years, the Robert E. Howard
Memorial Collection was forgotten at Howard Payne;
and the books were gradually placed on the open shelves
for general circulation. It was not until the recent
revival of the popularity of Howard's fiction that
interest was again shown in separating the Robert E.
Howard Memorial Collection from the rest of the Howard
Payne Library. With the intervention of forty years
much has been lost, but what we have been able to
reestablish is the result of the work of an enter-
prising reference librarian.

     When John Bloom, a reporter for the Dallas Times
Herald, asked the librarian, Mrs. Corrine Shields, for
help in researching an article on Robert E. Howard,
she began trying to locate the remnants of his collection. She first checked the shelf lists; but she found
that those did not begin until 1948, when the library
had stopped keeping accession lists.   She then
located the old accession lists in a dusty library
closet; but since the entries were not dated or
alphabetical, she could not determine which books were
in the Howard collection. Working from the information
in the June 29, 1936, Brownwood Bulletin, she knew
that a large part of the collection was history and
biography. Mrs. Shields went to the section of the
library where biographies are shelved and began to
pull books off the shelves to look for the bookplate
of "The Robert E. Howard Memorial Collection." After
several failures, she hit the jackpot with The Saga of
Billy the Kid by Walter Noble Burns. On the front
pastedown endpaper, was the bookplate and stamped inside
the book was the accession number. Armed with this
number, she went back to the dusty accession records

and found the book listed. She checked the preceding
and following books in the accession records and established a list of 268 books which were probably in the
original Howard collection. Checking first the card
catalog and then the books themselves, Mrs. Shields
found that many of the books are no longer in the
library and that some which are in the library do not
have the bookplate and therefore may be copies obtained
from another source.

Of the 268 books believed to have composed the
Robert E. Howard Memorial Collection, 45 remain with
the bookplate in place. All of these have remnants
of a blue slip of paper which was pasted on the back
free endpaper. This slip, which is intact in The
Saga of Billy the Kid, reads, "THIS BOOK IS FOR USE
IN THE LIBRARY." This evidence indicates that the
books were placed originally in a special collection
for library use only, as Dr. Howard had wished. Of
the 45 books, two contain inscriptions which show
that they were given to the library as memorial gifts
honoring Howard after his death. A few books contain
inscriptions or other evidence which indicate that they
actually belonged to Howard, but it is impossible to
determine exactly how many of the books were from his
own library and how many were added after his death.
Therefore I must be very careful in making assertions
about the influence of these books on Howard's writing,
but I can make a few interesting guesses.

Since nine of the 268 books are by Sir Arthur
Conan Doyle, he was probably one of Howard's favorite
authors. This admiration for Sir Arthur Conan Doyle
suggests a source for the name of Howard's most
popular character--Conan. Seven of the books are by
Talbot Mundy, and their presence on the list indicates
that the present publishers of Mundy's books are correct
in touting the similarity of his works to Howard's on
their book covers. Evidently, Howard read, admired,
and was influenced by Mundy's works.

I could formulate other guesses from the list, but
I will save them for the next issue of PQ. What follows
is an annotated checklist of the 45 books containing the
bookplate and which the Howard Payne Library now has.
The next three issues of PQ will have an alphabetical

listing of the books found on the accession list and
believed to have been in the Robert E. Memorial
Collection.

Annotated Checklist

Burns, Walter Noble. The Saga of Billy the Kid.
    Garden City, New York: Garden City Publishing
    Co., 1926.
Burroughs, Edgar Rice. The Beasts of Tarzan. New
    York: A.L. Burt Company, 1916.
    Stamped in blue ink on the verso of the front free
    endpaper is the name "ROBERT E. HOWARD," which
    indicates that the book originally belonged to
    him. On the back pastedown endpaper is the penciled
    signature, "Henry Potts."
Cabell, James Branch. The Cream of the Jest. New York:
    Modern Library, 1927.
Chesterton, Gilbert K. The Ballad of the White Horse.
    New York: Dood, Mead and Company, 1924.
Chidsey, Donald Barr. Sir Humphrey Gilbert, Elizabeth's
    Racketeer. New York: Harper and Brothers,
    Publishers, 1932.
    On p. 2 of this book, a paragraph is carefully
    underlined which might well have served as a
    description of one of Howard's own characters.
    "Contemporaries were fond of referring to
    'gentle Humphrey.' It is well not to be
    misled. The man was anything but 'gentle' in
    the modern sense of the word. He was a dreamer,
    yes, and a scholar; but he was also a man of
    action, who on the field of battle could be as
    brutal, as bloodthirsty, as any personage in
    history--far more so than most of them."
Cobb, Irvin S. Back Home, Being the Narrative of
    Judge Priest and His People. New York: George
    H. Doran Comapny, 1912.
    In this book, the bookplate of the Robert E. Howard
    Memorial Collection has been placed on top of a
    larger bookplate which reads, "THIS BOOK IS THE
    PROPERTY OF THE CROSS PLAINS CIRCULATING LIBRARY
    LOCATED AT THE CITY DRUG STORE."

Connor, Ralph. <u>Corporal Cameron of the North West Mounted Police</u>, <u>A Tale of the Macleod Trail</u>. New York: Grosset and Dunlap Publishers, . 1912.

The front free endpaper contains the ink inscription, "Robert E. Howard Jan. 22-1920."

Doyle, Sir Arthur Conan. <u>The Poison Belt</u>, <u>Being an Account of Another Amazing Adventure of Professor Challenger</u>. New York: George H. Doran Company, 1913.

In the lower left corner of the front pastedown endpaper is the stamp, "A.F. Bon Blon for Books Waco Texas." This book is the first of several which contain this stamp; its presence suggests that Howard had discovered a used book dealer in Waco, and frequented his store.

Dulles, Foster Rhea. <u>The Old China Trade</u>. Boston and New York: Houghton Mifflin Company, The Riverside Press Cambridge, 1930.

Some of the illustrations in this book would have been appropriate in Howard's own books. The following are from the list of illustrations: "The 'Boston' Taken by Savages at Nootka Sound," "Attack and Massacre of Crew of Ship 'Tonquin' by the Savages of the Northwest Coast," "A Chinese Opium Den," and "The Capture of Ting-Hai, Chusan."

Farnol, Jeffery. <u>Martin Conisby's Vengeance</u>. New York: A.L. Burt Company, 1921.

Penciled on the title-page is this statement. "Read 'Black Bartlemy's Treasure' first. This is a sequel to it."

Flinders, W.M., et. al. <u>The Book of History</u>, <u>A History of all Nations from the Earliest Times to the Present</u>. New York: The Grolier Society, and London: The Educational Book Co., [n.d.]

The set consists of twelve volumes. On the upper right corner of the front free endpaper is penciled the price, "12 vols. $20.00"

Foxcroft, Frank, ed. <u>War Verse</u>. New York: Thomas Y. Crowell Company, 1918.

Garnett, Richard. <u>The Twilight of the Gods and Other Tales</u>, with an introduction by T. E. Lawrence. New York: Alfred A. Knopf, 1926.

The above book has the following inscription on the half-title. "Inscribed in memory of| Robert E. Howard--|by a fellow writer who for years read and admired his stories--|Edmond Hamilton."

Gregg, Josiah. Commerce of the Prairies, The Journal of a Santa Fe Trader. Dallas, Texas: Southwest Press, 1933.

Hay, Thomas Robson. Hood's Tennessee Campaign. New York: Walter Neale Publisher, 1929.

Hemingway, Ernest. Winner Take Nothing. New York: Charles Scribner's Sons, 1933.
    The following inscription is on the front free endpaper. "To Bob--Dec. 25, 1933.|T[ruett] V[inson]."

Herbert, Sydney. The Fall of Feudalism in France. New York: Frederick A. Stokes Company, 1920.

Hobbs, Edward W. Sailing Ships at a Glance. New York and London: G. P. Putnam's Sons, The Knickerbocker Press, 1926.

House, Boyce. Were You in Ranger?.. Dallas, Texas: Tardy Publishing Company, Inc., 1935.
    On p. 46, a paragraph about a visit of Jess Willard, the world's heavyweight boxing champion, to Eastland County is underlined.

James, Marquis. They Had Their Hour. New York: Blue Ribbon Books, Inc., 1934.

Lamb, Harold. Tammerlane the Earth Shaker. New York: Robert M. McBride and Company, 1930.
    This stamp appears on the title-page. "A. F. Bon Blon| Rare Book Dealer| Waco, Texas."

Lawrence, T.E. Revolt in the Desert. Garden City, New York: Garden City Publishing Co., Inc., 1927.

London, Jack. The Valley of the Moon. New York: Grosset and Dunlap Publishers, 1916.

Lowell, Joan. The Cradle of the Deep. New York: Simon and Schuster, 1929.

March, Joseph Moncure. The Set-Up. New York: Covici, Friede, 1928.

Noyes, Alfred. Dick Turpin's Ride and Other Poems. New York: Frederick A. Stokes Company, 1927.

Paul, Louis. The Pumpkin Coach. New York: The Literary Guild, 1935.
    This book is inscribed on p. [i]. "This little

book is dedicated in kind memory of our deceased
friend Robert E. Howard. Mr. & Mrs. J. T.
McCarson Brownwood, Texas."

Rogers, Cameron. Drake's Quest. Garden City, New York:
Doubleday, Doran & Company, 1928.

Russell, Phillips. John Paul Jones: Man of Action.
New York: Blue Ribbon Books, 1930.
This stamp is on the title-page. "A.F. Bon Blon
Rare Book Dealer Waco, Texas."

Sayers, Dorothy, ed. The Omnibus of Crime. Garden City,
New York: Garden City Publishing Company, 1929.

Sinclair, Upton. Oil!. Long Beach, California: Published
by the Author, 1927.
There are many pencil underlinings in this book.
On p. 346, is the penciled statement, "We Jews
have learned not to go where we're new."

Sirango, Charles A. Riata and Spurs, The Story of a
Lifetime Spent in the Saddle as Cowboy and Ranger.
Boston and New York: Houghton Mifflin Company,
The Riverside Press Cambridge, 1931.
This book is stamped at the bottom of the title-
page, "A.F. Bon Blon Rare Book Dealers Waco, Texas."

Service, Robert W. The Pretender, A Story of the Latin
Quarter. New York: A.L. Burt Company, [n.d.].
This book is inscribed on the front free endpaper.
"My dear Sassoon: See the cuckoo in the tree
And when you see him think of me Rupert Brooke."

Service, Robert W. Ballads of a Bohemian. New York:
Barse and Hopkins, 1921.

Service, Robert W. Rhymes of a Redcross Man. New York:
Barse and Hopkins, 1916.

Service, Robert W. Rhymes of a Rolling Stone. New
York: Dodd, Mead and Company, 1923.

Service, Robert W. The Spell of the Yukon and Other
Verses. New York: Barse and Hopkins, 1907.

Stanley, Henry M. Wonders of the Tropics, or Explorations
and Adventures. [No place, date, or publisher is
given.] The verso of the title-page gives some
of this information, but the type is so battered
that it is illegible.

Thomas, Lowell. Beyond Khyber Pass into Forbidden
Afghanistan. New York: Grosset and Dunlap,
1925.

Thomas, Lowell. With Lawrence in Arabia. Garden City,
    New York: Garden City Publishing Company, 1924.
Voltaire. Zadig and Other Romances, Translated by
    H.I. Woolf and Wilfred S. Jackson. New York:
    Privately Printed for the Rarity Press, 1931.
Watson, Mrs. James. The Lower Rio Grande Valley of
    Texas, and Its Builders. Mission, Texas: Issued
    by The Lower Rio Grande Valley and Its Builders,
    Inc., 1931.
    This book is inscribed on the front free endpaper,
    "Mrs. James Watson|Mission|Texas. Pages [348-352]
    are blank pages with the heading "Autographs."
    Page [348] contains three signatures: "Richard
    Davis,|Robert J. Moore,|David M. King--Rio Hondo."
White, Owen P. Lead and Likker. New York: Minton,
    Balch and Company, 1932.
Witwer, H. C. The Leather Pushers. New York: Grosset
    and Dunlap, 1921.
    The title-page gives the following information
    about the book. "Illustrated with scenes from
    the photoplay The Universal--Jewel--Collier's
    Series of Romances of the Ring."
    The front free endpaper contains the following
    inscription. "To--R.E.H.| in memory of the|summer
    of 1927--in|which we decide upon|the fact that
    we are|economicially [sic] and intellectually
    superior|and etc! Also don't|forget our opinions
    on|other subjects ranging|from prizefighting to|
    birth control!| T[ruett] V[inson]|June 27 1927--"
Yeats, William B., ed. Irish Fairy and Folk Tales.
    New York: The Modern Library, [n.d.].
    On the title-page is the following stamp. "A.F.
    Bon Blon|Rare Book Dealer|Waco, Texas."

NEW BOOK RELEASED ABOUT ROBERT E. HOWARD
Reviewed by Tevis Clyde Smith

Donald M. Grant, Publisher, West Kingston, Rhode Island 02892, has just released Glenn Lord's Bio-Bibliography of Robert Ervin Howard, The Last Celt, a marvelous book which retails for $20. The book is a real value at the price.

It involved many years work on the part of Mr. Lord, the Editor and Compiler. If you are a Howard enthusiast the book is for you; if you are unacquainted with Bob it will whet your appetite for the Howard books which are listed.

Bob Howard was born in 1906 and died in 1936. He lived most of his life in Cross Plains, but spent his senior year at Brownwood High, and later attended business school at Howard Payne. He was a brilliant writer and a fascinating conversationalist.

He worked hard; and aimed his writing at the pulp trade. His principal market for many years was Weird Tales. Farnsworth Wright, the editor, accepted Spear and Fang in the mid-twenties, and after a period of several months began to publish Howard with regularity. Bob was a prolific writer and did not confine himself to the supernatural, as he also wrote for western magazines, as well as producing fight fiction, spicy stories, poetry, and at least one article for a trade journal. He is now at the peak of his popularity, and translations of his work have been printed in France, The Netherlands, Spain, Germany, and Japan. He has also been published in Canada and Britain. I am happy to state that I became acquainted with Bob in 1923, and that Donald Grant published one book which we co-authored. The title is Red Blades of Black Cathay. It is now out of print in its original form of introduction and three stories but the story from which the book takes its name has recently been included in Zebra's The Book of Robert E. Howard, Volume I, and has had local distribution at a supermarket and a drug store.

Jonathan Bacon, P.O. Box 147, Lamoni, Iowa 50140 carries a good stock of Howard in print books and

gives prompt and efficient service. He will send a
brochure and prices for a self-addressed stamped
envelope.

Copyright ©1976 by Tevis Clyde Smith. All
rights reserved.

This review was first published in Vol. 1, number
3, Pecan Valley News, Tuesday, September 7, 1976, and
is reproduced in this issue of Paperback Quarterly
with my approval. To bring the article up to date and
to fit in with its appearance in this journal, I should
mention that The Last Celt is now in an attractive
paperback edition by arrangement with Glen Lord and
the original publisher, Donald M. Grant. The new edition, marked at $5.95, is a Berkley Windhover book
published by Berkley Publishing Corporation.

Jonathan Bacon still advertises the original
edition in his current catalogue. Jonathan has a new
address: Jonathan Bacon, Stygian Isle Press, Fantasy
Crossroads, Box 12428, Shawnee Mission, Kansas, 66212.
The Knowledge Shop, 1500 Austin Avenue, Brownwood,
Texas 76801, is also interested in Howard books. It
is worthwhile for the book purchaser to get acquainted
with both of these dealers.

The Last Celt is a real tribute to Bob Howard:
part autobiography, part biography, part bibliography.
Your Howard collection is incomplete without it.

T.C.S.

PAPERBACKS ON REVIEW

Great Action Stories
Edited by William Kittredge & Steven M. Krauzer
(Mentor Books, May 1977) 308 pp. $1.50

One of the earliest forms of the paperback original
was the anthology. A new and very entertaining anthology
is Great Action Stories. Even though two stories (Fredric Brown's "Arena" and Dashiell Hammett's "The Gutting
of Couffignal") may be overly familiar to fans of science
fiction and detective fiction, respectively, there's no
denying that they are great action stories. Besides,
the book reprints for the first time Mickey Spillane's
"I'll Die Tomorrow," which makes amends. Also included
are such gems as "Cyclists' Raid" (retitled "The Wild
One' for the famous movie based on it), Richard Math-
eson's "Duel" (another famous movie tie-in), and William Harrison's "Roller Ball Murder" (from which was
derived a not-so-famous film). This is a far from
definitive listing of contents; the book is over 300
pages long and a bargain at the price. But what I
like best was the "Introduction" by the editors, in
which they define what they mean by the term "action
stories" and show how each story in the book meets their
criteria. These comments alone make the book a must
for anyone interested in the field.

----Bill Crider

The Menacers
by Donald Hamilton
(Fawcett Gold Medal, 1968) 192 pp.

The eleventh Matt Helm adventure could have been
called "Matt Helm vs. The Flying Saucers." While not
quite as bad as the Dean Martin Helm movie with the same
theme, it's still a pretty poor effort. Helm is called
in to escort Annette O'Leary to Los Alamos, where she
can be grilled about the flying saucer (with USAF mark-
ings!) she claims to have seen. If anyone should threaten

to kidnap O'Leary, Helm has orders to shoot her immediately. And there <u>are</u> agents out to prevent Helm's
trip; Vady, the Russian secret agent who alternately
falls in love with and shoots Helm is back, accompanied
by Harsek, the Mad Czech. Several operatives from another American agency also do their best to block Helm,
plus themselves, with typical bureaucratic snafus.

   This novel is easily the worst in this series since
the abysmal fourth novel, <u>The Silencers</u>. Hamilton is
trapped in his own formula, and has a very hard time
getting out of it. The kidnappings, betrayals, turn-
coatery, and double-agent escapades are all old hat by
now; there is little suspense and less adventure here.
At one point there is even a poison-gas-in-the-closed-
car episode, which even Helm admits is too James-Bondsy.
<u>The Menacers</u> isn't boring, mind you--just routine.
<u>Very</u> routine. (C)

                              ----Martin Morse Wooster

<u>The Night Creature</u>
by Brian Ball
(Fawcett Gold Medal, 1974) 159 pp. $0.95.

   Book publishing is like television: success
breeds imitation. After the huge paperback sales of
<u>Rosemary's Baby</u> and <u>The Exorcist</u> it was inevitable that
modern horror novels would proliferate, not only in hard
covers but also in original paperbacks. One such book
is <u>The Night Creature</u> by Brian Ball. The book's original
title is given on the cover as <u>The Venomous Serpent</u>, but
the publishers give no indication as to where that title
was used. It is possible that the book appeared under
that title in Britain and that Fawcett's is the first
printing in this country, hence the "Gold Medal" desig-
nation (usually reserved for original editions). At
any rate, the book is very brief, more novellette than
novel length, having only 159 pages, many of them blank
or chapter ends. The reader should not expect a concen-
tration of horrors, but rather a fast-moving, well-
written study in terror.

                              ----Bill Crider

The Creeping Death
by Maxwell Grant
(Pyramid Books, May 1977) 144 pp. $1.25

Who knows what evil lurks in the hearts of men?
The Shadow knows, and Pyramid's Shadow book #14, The
Creeping Death, is no exception. Originally published
in The Shadow Magazine vol. IV, number 4, January
15, 1933, The Creeping Death, like other Shadow stories
the last few years, is being re-issued.

In a 15 year period, Maxwell Grant (pseudonym for
Walter B. Gibson) wrote more than 275 short novels of
The Shadow which originally appeared in The Shadow
Magazine and formed the basis for the popular radio
program featuring Lamont Cranston as The Shadow.

In The Creeping Death, The Shadow tangles with an
eccentric scientist who is making and trading synthetic
gold for real gold reserves around the world. His attempt to gain wealth is linked to a "mad" obsession for
power and ultimately control of the world. Walter B.
Gibson weaves a plot of human greed and double-cross
around a mysterious creeping death which appears hope-
less even for The Shadow.

Though short (144 pages), like all shadow books
this one is full of pleasure for those who love good
vs. evil plots. And though enjoyable, I would have
bought this one just for its remarkable cover illus-
tration by "Steranko."

---Billy C. Lee

The Prey
by Robert Arthur Smith
(Fawcett Gold Medal, 1977) $1.95

The Prey is given as the title of this book on the
cover and title page. On the copyright page, however,
the title is given as Prey of the Werewolves, which is
more revealing of the contents than is The Prey.
This is a book in the grand tradition of gothics---the
discovered manuscript, the tales within the tale, the
18th century setting, all are here. All this, plus a

surfeit of horrors for the connoisseur; almost every
page seems bespattered with the gore of dismembered
bodies, the risen dead, the undying. Trapped in this
maelstrom of terror is Albrecht Morivania Von Dunkel-
feuer und Molgenherz (just call him Morivania for short).
In the nearly 450 pages of this novel he undergoes more
fainting spells, blackouts, evil summonses and near
concussions than any hero in years. He's even thrown
in the Bastille! The fact that he seems incredibly
dense about the cause of all the goings-on can only be
attributed to the fact that he failed to read the copyright page. Or possibly he is less sophisticated about
werewolves than modern readers. Occasionally one wants
to reach out and shake him. But that doesn't really
detract from the fun of this totally preposterous novel.
No one is going to believe a word of it even for a
minute, but no one who has enjoyed The Monk or Melmoth
The Wanderer should miss it; it's a treat in its own
way and not the kind of thing you find being done these
days, much less being done well.

                              ----Bill Crider

Cumulative Paperback Index 1939-1959
by R. Reginald and M.R. Burgess
(Gale Research Co.) $35 1973

   Probably the most useful research aid to the paperback collector interested in the 1939 to 1959 period is
the Cumulative Paperback Index 1939-1959. Its 362 pages
consist of 14,051 book entries alphabetically arranged
by author and by title and giving publisher, book number,
date of publication, and price. Pages XIII to XXIV give
a run down of the publishers specifications including
address, stock number spans, book height, book edge color,
numbering system, price code, and total books published
or recorded. There is a total number of 33 publishers
issued under 69 imprints.
   The publishers price is $35.00 but if you include
payment with your order, you can deduct 5% making it
only $33.25. The Address is: Gale Research Co., Book
Tower, Detroit, Mich. 44226. It's expensive but well
worth the price.

   It is interesting to note that R. Reginald and
M.R. Burgess are one and the same person. Michael
Burgess is a librarian at California State College, San
Bernardino, California. When he leaves his librarian
job, he assumes the name Robert Reginald for professional
use as an editor, publisher, and author. It seems
justifiable for Burgess to use pseudonyms when one
examines the number of books and magazines he has
edited, published, and written in the last eight years
in his spare time only. It's not plausible for just
one person to accomplish so much while holding a full
time job. R. Reginald is mostly involved in paperbacks
or books about paperbacks of which CPI is a prime example. He began collecting paperbacks in 1964 when he
found that the local public library in Spokane, Washing-
ton had very few science fiction and fantasy books to
offer. He began buying used science fiction and fantasy
paperbacks. That was 14 years ago and he now has over
16,000 books all but a few hundred of which are paperbacks. In a recent letter, he says "Much of my collection consists of science fiction and fantasy material,

but I also acquire pbs of historical interest, and have made some effort to pick up unusual items (like the first books in a particular number system)."

M.R. Burgess as R. Reginald, C. Everett Cooper, Lucas Webb, and himself has at the age of thirty the following credits:

1a. *Stella Nova: The Contemporary Science Fiction Authors*. Unicorn & Son, Los Angeles, 1970. (108 copies issued privately)

1b. retitled and slightly revised: *Contemporary Science Fiction Authors, First Edition*. Arno Press, 1975.

2. *Cumulative Paperback Index, 1939-1959*. Gale Research Company, 1973.

3. *Ancestral Voices; an Anthology of Early Science Fiction*. Arno Press, 1975 (edited with Douglas Menville).

4. *The Attempted Assassination of John F. Kennedy; a Political Fantasy*. Borgo Press, 1976 (as Lucas Webb).

5. *Ancient Hauntings*. Arno Press, 1976 (edited with Douglas Menville).

6. *Phantasmagoria*. Arno Press, 1976 (edited with Douglas Menville).

7. *R.I.P.; Five Stories of the Supernatural*. Arno Press, 1976 (edited with Douglas Menville).

8. *The Spectre Bridegroom, and Other Horrors*. Arno Press, 1976 (edited with Douglas Menville).

9. *Up Your Asteroid! A Science Fiction Farce*. Borgo Press, 1977 (as C. Everett Cooper).

10. *Things to Come; an Illustrated History of the Science Fiction Film*. Times Books, 1977 (edited with Douglas Menville).

11. *King Solomon's Children; Some Parodies of H. Rider Haggard*. Arno Press, June 1978 (edited with Douglas Menville).

12. *Dreamers of Dreams; an Anthology of Fantasy*. Arno Press, June 1978 (edited with Douglas Menville).

13. *They; Three Parodies of H. Rider Haggard's She*. Arno Press, June 1978 (edited with Douglas Menville; includes a special introduction delineating the

bibliographic puzzles behind the Haggard parodies).

14. *Worlds of Never; Three Fantastic Novels.* Arno Press, June 1978 (edited with Douglas Menville).

15. *Science Fiction and Fantasy Literature; a Checklist; with Contemporary Science Fiction Authors* II. Gale Research Company, July/September 1978.

16. *Hulke's Analytical Congressional Directory, First Edition.* Forthcoming, April 1979 (compiled by Malcolm Hulke and R. Reginald).

17. *The Light in the Window; a Bio-bibliography of of the Gothic Romance.* Forthcoming, 1979.

18. An illustrated history of special effects in motion pictures, co-authored with Paul Kraus, Forthcoming, 1978/79.

19. A complete revision of the *Cumulative Paperback Index,* 1979/80.

Other credits: Associate Editor, *Forgotten Fantasy* magazine, Oct. 1970–June 1971 (all issues published); Co-Editor, Newcastle Publishing Co., Inc., 1971-Date; Editor, *Forgotten Fantasy Library,* 1973-Date; Advisory Editor (with Douglas Menville), *Arno Press Science Fiction Series,* 1975; Advisory Editor (with Douglas Menville), *Arno Press Supernatural and Occult Fiction Series,* 1976; Advisory Editor (with Douglas Menville) *Arno Press Lost Race And Adult Fantasy Fiction Series,* 6/78; Publisher, Borgo Press*, 1975-Date; Contributing Editor, *Contemporary Authors,* 1977-Date; three articles in *The People's Almanac II;* currently working on four articles for *The Book of Lists II,* edited by Irving Wallace and group.

-----Billy C. Lee

*In a future issue, the PQ will feature an article on the Borgo Press.

Notes & Queries

1. A particularly interesting Gold Medal Book is #129,
Mansion of Evil (1950), by Joseph Millard. Its outward
appearance is that of any other early Gold Medal original, except that the cover is drawn in comic book style.
The cover blurb announces "Something New! A complete
novel in words and pictures. A thrill on every page."
Inside is indeed a complete novel in color comic strip
drawings. Was this an early Gold Medal experiment,
attempting to appeal to readers of comics? Was the
experiment repeated? Was Joseph Millard both author
and artist? The editors of PQ hope that any reader
having the answer to these questions will let them
know.

2. Pseudonyms are always fun. In 1964, Gold Medal
Books published No Way to Treat a Lady by "Harry
Longbaugh." When the movie version of the book appeared
in 1968, Gold Medal reprinted the text under the author's
real name: William Goldman. And in 1969, Bantam pub-
lished (as an original) Goldman's screenplay, Butch
Cassidy and the Sundance Kid. The real name of the
Sundance Kid was, you guessed it, Harry Longbaugh.

3. Everyone who collects Dell paperbacks have noticed
how the number of pages in each book are often the same.
Just for fun, I randomly (scientifically as possible)
chose 100 Dell paperbacks from the first 1000 stock
numbers. This is what I found:

>   44% had 192 pages
>   23% had 240 pages
>   16% had 224 pages
>   10% had 256 pages
>   5% had 288 pages
>   1% had 320 pages
>   1% had 144 pages

Of course since this represents only 10% of the total
1000 books, its accuracy remains to be seen. Assuming

the percentages are semi-accurate then 440 out of 1000 have 192 pages, 230 out of 1000 have 240 pages, 160 out of 1000 have 224 pages, 100 out of 1000 have 256 pages, 50 out of 1000 have 288 pages, etc...(In such a small sample, the 1%'s are not significant at all). Why did Dell do this? It probably had to do with ease of printing or perhaps control of cost in printing. Does anyone know? Someone repeat this experiment to see if the 44%, 23%, 16%, 10%, and 5% hold up. Perhaps someone lucky enough to have a complete set (1-1000) and having lots of time could give us a complete breakdown.

4. According to an advertisement at the back of Avon book #384 (Louis Beretti by Donald Henderson Clarke), Jack Woodford's Dangerous Love, The Abortive Hussy, The Hard-boiled Virgin, The Rites of Love, Untamed Darling, Ecstasy Girl, Free Lovers, Grounds for Divorce, Male and Female, Passionate Princess, Peeping Tom, Teach Me to Love, and Three Gorgeous Hussies were available through Avon Publishing Co. These are all the books which are credited to Jack Woodford in the Cumulative Paperback Index 1939-1959 by R. Reginald and M.R. Burgess. According to CPI however, the first five listed above were Avon publications and the remaining eight were Novel Library publications. Moreover, two of the Avon books, Untamed Darling Avon #297 and #403 and The Rites of Love Avon #409, according to the book ad were 35¢ each but the CPI indicates 25¢ each. Can anyone clear up this riddle?

5. At first glance, one might think I own two copies of Conan The Avenger by Robert E. Howard, Bjorn Nyberg, and L. Sprague De Camp (Ace Conan Book #10). The truth is I don't own a copy of Conan The Avenger at all--- or at least not a complete copy. I do have two books with the Conan The Avenger cover but once inside, the story changes...literally. One copy indeed has the "Avenger" title page and provides an exiting "Avenger" story until page 162, where without warning becomes the 195th page of Conan The Conqueror (Ace Conan Book #9).

It remains <u>Conan The Conqueror</u> until the end of the book on page 224 (<u>Conan The Avenger</u> is supposed to have 192 pages).

The other copy also has "The Avenger" cover, but the title page is <u>Conan The Conqueror</u> which it remains until page 34. This time with no warning of page number inconsistences, the 35th page becomes <u>Conan The Avenger</u> and remains such until the end of the book on page 192. Apparently the paperback binder really goofed!

WANTED:

Armed Services Editions
Avon Fantasy Monthly
Avon Mystery Monthly
Hillman publications (books or digests)
Books by or edited by Donald Wollheim
Ace edition of Tolkien's <u>Lord of the Rings</u> trilogy
    and <u>The Hobbit</u> (1965)
Ballantine edition of Tolkien's <u>Lord of the Ring</u>
    trilogy and <u>The Hobbit</u> (first printing)
Books by L. Sprague De Camp before 1968
Croydon Mystery digests
<u>Manhunt</u> magazine 1950's
Books by Poul Anderson before 1960
Books by Rex Stout before 1950
Books by Leslie Charteris before 1950
Ace double #D-36

A. Taylor
P.O Box 547
Brownwood, Texas 76801

William H. Lyles
13810 Castle Rho. #304
Silver Spring, MD 20904

phone-(301) 890-6412

WANT LIST: DELL PAPERBACKS

25¢ MAPBACKS: 9, 11, 38, 73, 77, 89, 152, 205, 278, 359, 421, 434, 613, 630, 642, 667, 707, 711, 725 (2nd, 3rd, 5th printings), 832, 847 (2nd, 3rd, 4th, 5th printings), 875, 879, 883, 930, 935, 938, 963, 976 (2nd, 3rd printings), 979, 993

25¢ MAPBACK reprints: any except: 1333, 1339, 1341, 1348, 1366, 1386, 1388, 1402, 1407, 1434, 1440, 1492, 1533, 1534, 1542, 1590.

10¢ BOOKS: 3, 11, 13, 14, 17, 18, 25, 28, 29, 31, 33, 35

"D" 35¢ books: D105, D112, D119, D120, D135, D155, D162, D164, D169, D198, D227, D236, D240, D332, D337, D350, D364, D365, D382, D395, D402, D427, D447, D457

"F" 50¢ books: F51, F64, F132, F142, F144, F156, F179, F186

"R" 40¢ books: R119

"X" 75¢ books: X1, X8 (19th printing or later)

"Y" 95¢ books: Y001 (2nd printing, tie-in with movie Camelot)

Dell First Editions: 8, 11, 60, 64, 65, 89, 91, 93, 108

First Editions "A" 25¢ series: A110, A123, A124, A125, A129, A131, A134, A135, A138, A147, A148, A151, A157, A171, A173, A209, any 2nd printings

First Editions "B" 35¢ series: B106, B113, B117, B131, B132, B133, B134, B139, B147, B149, B161, B164, B171, B181, B194, B197, B199, B203, B209, B215

First Editions "C" 50¢ series: C112, C113

Laurel "LB" 35¢ series: LB144, LB153

Laurel "LC" 50¢ series: LC104, LC106, LC111, LC112, LC115, LC123, LC124, LC125, LC129

Laurel "LS" 60¢ series: LS102, LS103, LS106

Laurel "LX" 75¢ series: LX132

Laurel "LY" 95¢ series: LY109, LY110

Dell Visual Books: VY4

Other Wants:
---Dell Special Student Editions: any except 2nd printing of "The Yellow Room"
---Dell digest-sized comic-book version of George Harmon Coxe's "Four Frightened Women" (or others in this series)
---issues of "Zane Grey's Western Magazine" (I have too few to list), "Luke Short's Western Magazine," or "Dell Mystery Novels" (except No. 1)
---any other Dell digest-sized magazines
---any Dell one-shot un-numbered publications (digest-sized) except "Jungle Belles" and "Hopalong Cassidy"
---any un-numbered Dell paperbacks except "Dick Tracy and the Woo-Woo Sisters" and "Blondie and Dagwood in Footlight Folly"
---any copies with Paris Belt ad on back cover except 1000 and 1002
---any Dell paperbacks with dust jackets

I MAINTAIN A TRADING STOCK OF OVER 1,000 TITLES, INCLUDING DELLS, AVONS, OTHER EARLY PAPERBACKS; HARBACK MYSTERIES, ETC. OF COURSE, I WILL BUY OUTRIGHT ANYTHING ON MY WANT LIST. If you have any of the really scarce items (Crossword Puzzle Books/Joke Books), please contact me: I will pay top dollar.

LORE-X

Published Quarterly

by

Martin E. Gottschalk
P. O. Box 851
Brownwood, Texas 76801

Editor

Bill Crider, Ph.D., Howard Payne University, Brownwood

Associate Editors

Lewis H. Miller, D.D., LL.D., 910 8th, Brownwood
Charlotte Laughlin, Ph.D., Howard Payne University, Brownwood
Elva Dobson, Poet, 2103 11th, Brownwood

Subscription Rates

Annual $5.00; Single copies $1.75

Correspondence and subscriptions should be sent to the publisher. Contributions of prose, verse and artwork will be considered which reflect the American culture. Manuscripts must be typewritten, up to twentyfive hundred words, double spaced and original, although any reasonable length will be considered. They should be addressed to the editor with the above address.

The purpose of this journal is to provide a medium for individuals who are devoted to the arts and humanities so that they may have an opportunity to express themselves and share with others.

www.ingramcontent.com/pod-product-compliance
Lightning Source LLC
Chambersburg PA
CBHW021118020426
42331CB00004B/544